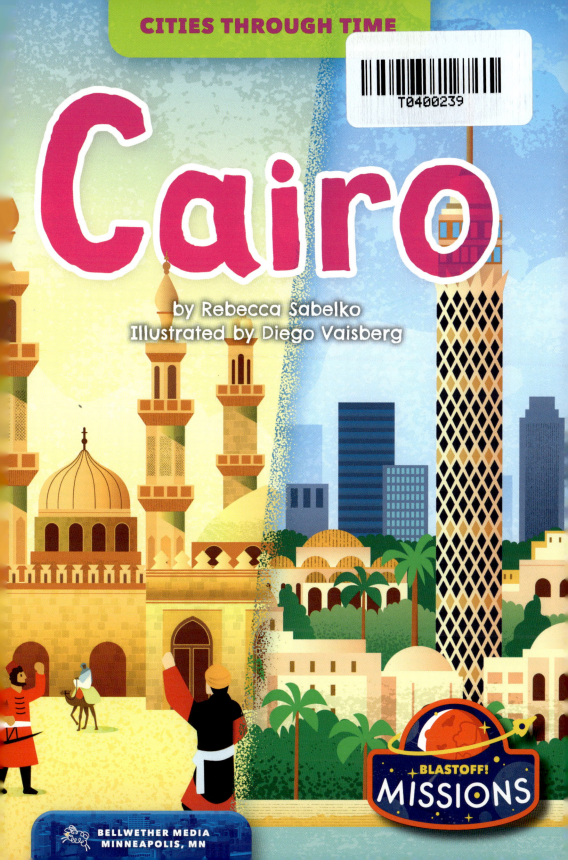

Blastoff! Missions takes you on a learning adventure! Colorful illustrations and exciting narratives highlight cool facts about our world and beyond. Read the mission goals and follow the narrative to gain knowledge, build reading skills, and have fun!

Traditional Nonfiction

Narrative Nonfiction

Blastoff! Universe

MISSION GOALS

> FIND YOUR SIGHT WORDS IN THE BOOK.

> LEARN ABOUT DIFFERENT PERIODS IN CAIRO'S HISTORY.

> LEARN ABOUT WHICH GROUPS HAVE CONTROLLED CAIRO IN THE PAST.

This edition first published in 2025 by Bellwether Media, Inc.

No part of this publication may be reproduced in whole or in part without written permission of the publisher. For information regarding permission, write to Bellwether Media, Inc., Attention: Permissions Department, 6012 Blue Circle Drive, Minnetonka, MN 55343.

Library of Congress Cataloging-in-Publication Data

LC record for Cairo available at: https://lccn.loc.gov/2024021460

Text copyright © 2025 by Bellwether Media, Inc. BLASTOFF! MISSIONS and associated logos are trademarks and/or registered trademarks of Bellwether Media, Inc. Bellwether Media is a division of Chrysalis Education Group.

Editor: Christina Leaf   Designer: Laura Sowers

Printed in the United States of America, North Mankato, MN.

This is **Blastoff Jimmy**! He is here to help you on your mission and share fun facts along the way!

Table of Contents

Welcome to Cairo!	4
A Growing City	6
Modern Changes	16
The City Today	20
Glossary	22
To Learn More	23
Beyond the Mission	24
Index	24

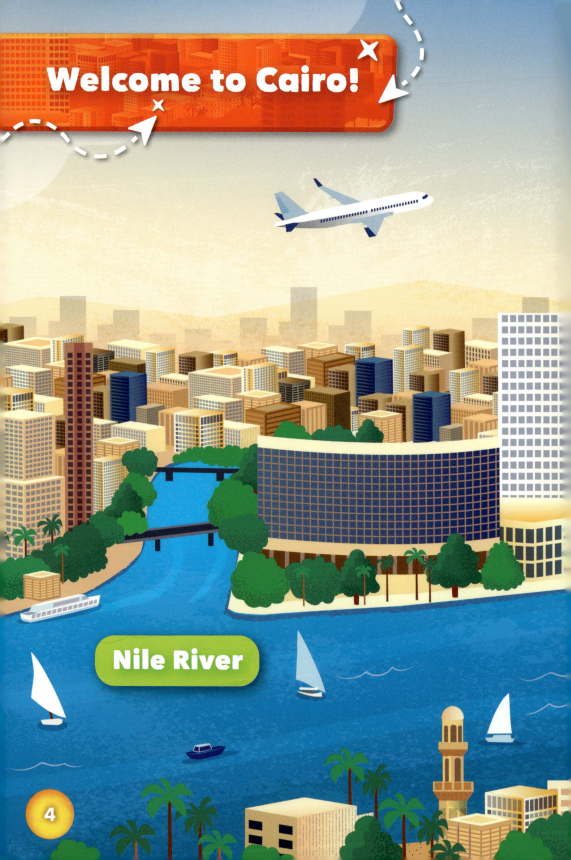

Welcome to one of the largest cities in Africa! Cairo, Egypt, sits along the Nile River. This busy city has a long history.

Let's explore the many changes it has seen!

A Growing City

around 2500 BCE

The Nile is having its yearly flood. Farmers cannot tend to their fields.

Here comes Rome's **emperor**! He is here to see the land he now rules. He passes the **Fortress** of Babylon. It stands at the tip of the Nile River **delta**.

emperor

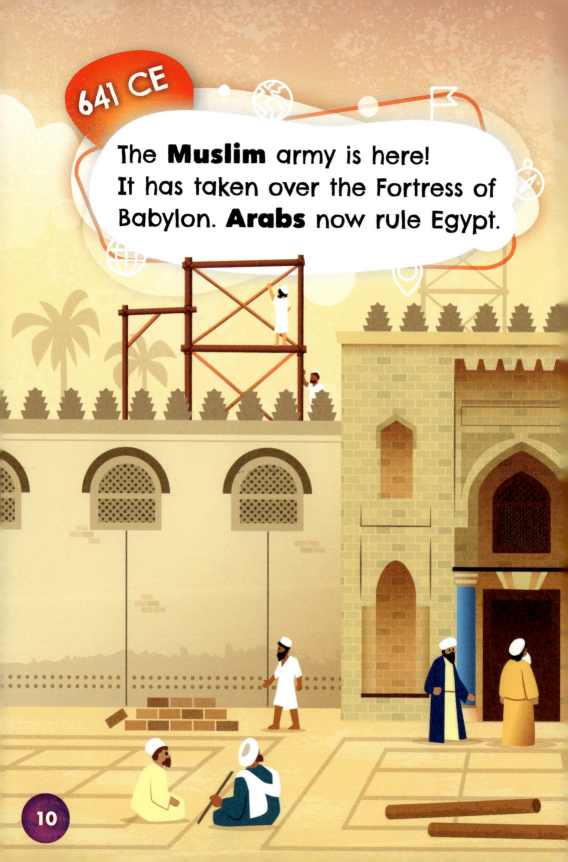

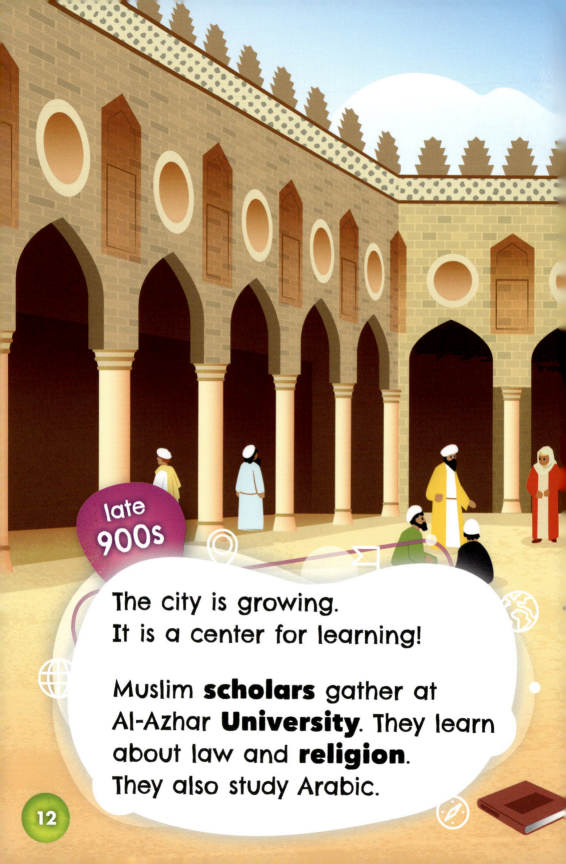

late 900s

The city is growing. It is a center for learning!

Muslim **scholars** gather at Al-Azhar **University**. They learn about law and **religion**. They also study Arabic.

around 1340

Cairo is busy! Nearly half a million people live here.

The **spice trade** brings many travelers. They trade goods throughout the city's streets.

Modern Changes

late 1800s

Cairo looks different! Leaders used money from Europe to create city squares. They built grand gardens and buildings.

But they cannot pay back the money they borrowed. Great Britain gets ready to take control.

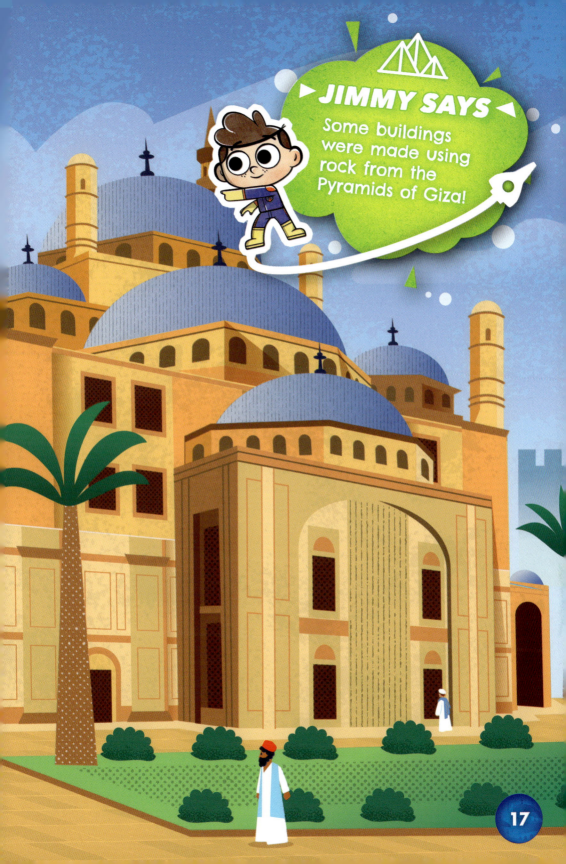

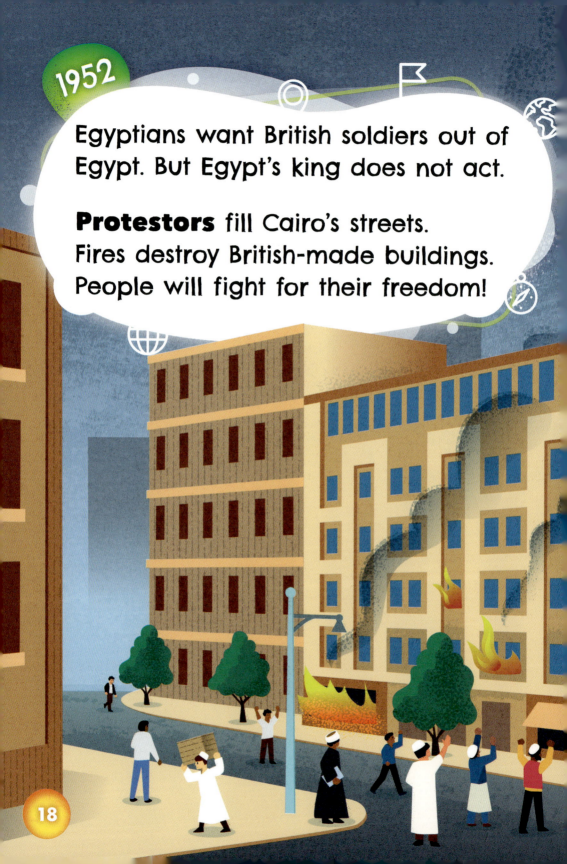

The City Today

Over 20 million people live in and around Cairo. Cars and buses honk from the streets. Mosques and museums welcome visitors.

Cairo mixes the old world with the new!

Cairo Timeline

around 2500 BCE: The Pyramid of Menkaure, the third pyramid at Giza, is built

around 30 BCE: Roman Emperor Augustus visits the Fortress of Babylon in Roman-controlled Egypt

641 CE: Egypt's first mosque, Amr ibn al-As, is built

late 900s: Al-Azhar University is built

around 1340: Cairo is an important stop in the world spice trade

late 1800s: Great Britain occupies Egypt

1952: The Cairo Fire is a result of protests from the British army attacking Cairo police

Cairo, Egypt

Glossary

Arabs–people who mostly live in the Middle East and northern Africa

delta–the land at the mouth of a river

emperor–a ruler

fortress–a building or place from which people can prevent attacks

mosque–a building that Muslims use for worship

Muslim–related to people of the Islamic faith; Muslims follow the teachings of the Prophet Muhammad as told to him from Allah.

pharaoh–a ruler of Egypt from long ago

protestors–people who show they are against something

religion–a set of beliefs, often about a god or gods

scholars–people who are very educated and often study a particular subject

spice trade–the buying and selling of spices between Asia and Europe

university–a school that people go to after high school

To Learn More

AT THE LIBRARY

Davies, Monika. *Egypt*. Minneapolis, Minn.: Bellwether Media, 2023.

Dean, Jessica. *Egypt*. Minneapolis, Minn.: Jump!, 2019.

Leaf, Christina. *Rome*. Minneapolis, Minn.: Bellwether Media, 2024.

ON THE WEB

FACTSURFER

Factsurfer.com gives you a safe, fun way to find more information.

1. Go to www.factsurfer.com.

2. Enter "Cairo" into the search box and click 🔍.

3. Select your book cover to see a list of related content.

BEYOND THE MISSION

> WHAT FACT FROM THE BOOK DID YOU THINK WAS THE MOST INTERESTING?

> IF YOU WERE A SCHOLAR, WHAT WOULD YOU STUDY? WHY?

> IF YOU WERE GOING TO CREATE A CITY SQUARE IN CAIRO, WHAT WOULD YOU INCLUDE? DRAW A PICTURE.

Index

Africa, 5
Al-Azhar University, 12
Arabs, 10, 11, 12
city squares, 16
Cleopatra, 8
Egypt, 5, 8, 10, 11, 18
emperor, 9
Europe, 16
fires, 18
flood, 6
Fortress of Babylon, 8, 9, 10
Giza, 7, 17

Great Britain, 16, 18
mosque, 11, 20
museums, 20
Muslim army, 10
Nile River, 4, 5, 6, 9
people, 14, 18, 20
pharaoh, 7
protestors, 18, 19
pyramid, 7, 17
Rome, 8, 9
scholars, 12, 13
spice trade, 14
timeline, 21